Joy's Annoying Toys

Clive Gifford

Illustrated by Susie Thomas

Letts

Joy Royal owned a shop called Toys Ahoy!
It was very popular with crowds of girls and boys.

Joy sold noisy toys like stuffed wolves, which howled. She sold juggling clubs, bouncing balls and smiling owls and cows.

But three boys didn't enjoy the toys they bought from Joy.
They returned the toys to Joy, saying that they were annoying.

Joy vowed to fix the toys and toiled all night.
She uncoiled wires, squirted oil, but nothing seemed right.

In the morning, Joy sighed.
Her work had been foiled.
It was very annoying.
These three toys were spoiled.

Can you draw a line between the pairs of words which rhyme?

uncoil	enjoy
boy	power
choice	point
android	boil
joint	frown
town	toys
flower	voice
noise	avoid

3

First, there was a ball that wouldn't bounce at all.
Then, there was a cuddly owl, who did nothing but scowl.
Worse than the scowling owl, was a little brown cow.
A "moo" noise should have sounded when you touched the cow,
but this cow went, "oink", "meow" or "bow-wow"!

"Boy, you spoilt toys are annoying me!"
Joy cried.
"You have left me no choice,"
she said, picking up the phone.

Joy avoided clowns,
as she found them silly and **LOUD**.
When she was young,
she'd enjoyed their clowning around.
Now Joy had no choice
but to call Clown Town.
The toys could only be saved
by the power of a clown.

The letters oo can sound short, as in hood, or they can sound long, as in room. Say each word below and write either short or long beside it, according to the sound the oo makes.

pool _____

crook _____

good _____

shook _____

soon _____

loose _____

soot _____

stood _____

tooth _____

school _____

5

"Hello, this is Joy Royal from Toys Ahoy!" she said. "I have some annoying toys here – can you help?"

Joy heard a yawning noise down the phone.

"A h h h h h. Hi Joy, I'm Drowsy, here in Clown Town. The other clowns are out, and I need a nap now."

"How can you sleep when annoying toys are around?" asked Joy.

"Well, I'm rather scared of rowdy toys." Drowsy's voice sounded nervous.

"They're not rowdy, you coward!" frowned Joy. "Annoying toys cannot be enjoyed by girls and boys. Look, I don't want a row, but you'd better come down here, **NOW**!"

Adjectives are words which describe things. Can you circle each of the adjectives in the sentences below?

Joy sold noisy toys.

The spoilt toys annoyed Joy.

There was a cuddly owl.

I'm scared of rowdy toys.

He fell asleep telling his own poor jokes.

There was a tiny bag of powder inside it.

Drowsy mopped up the slimy custard with a towel.

In a daze, he tripped over the brown cow.

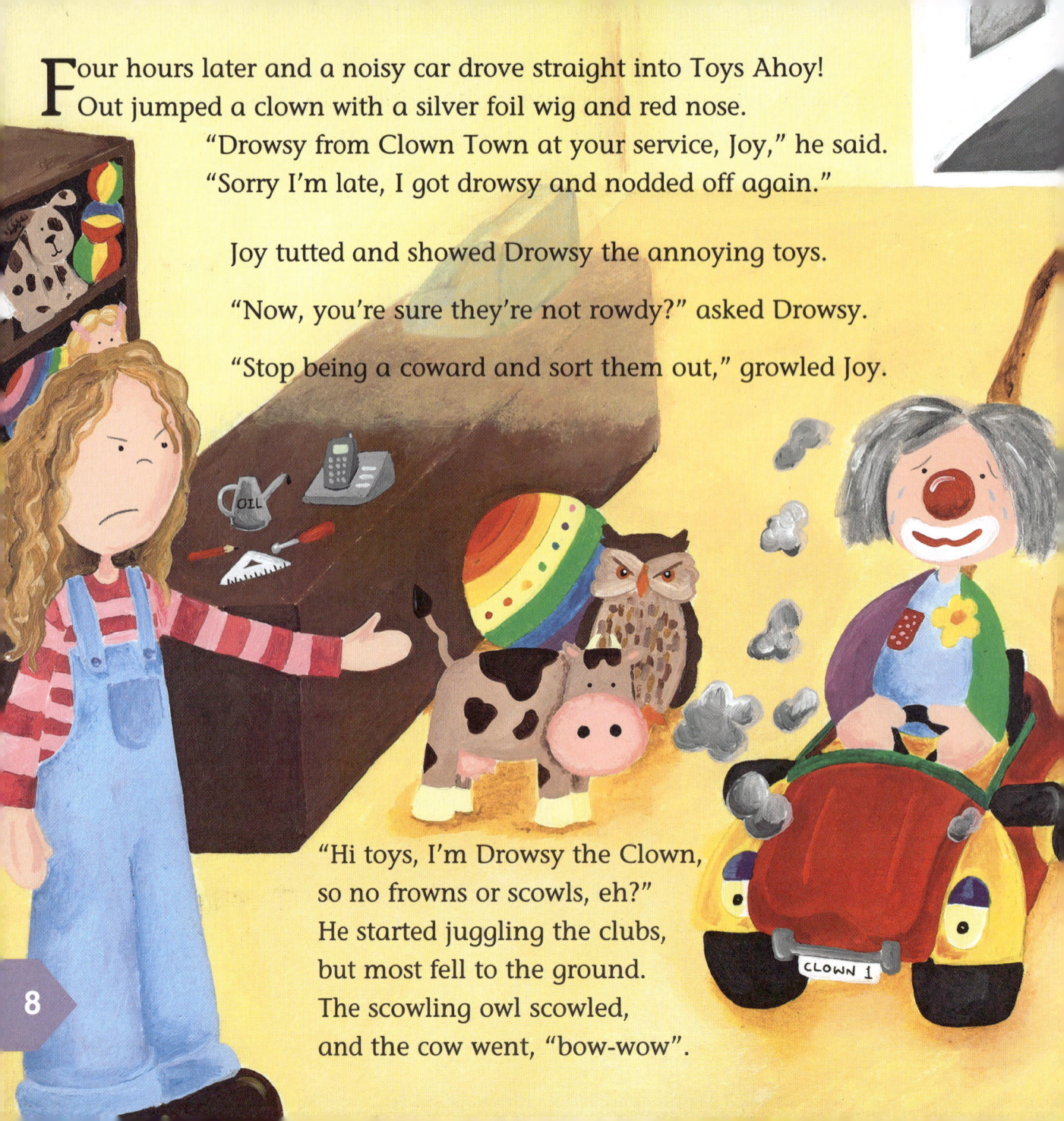

Four hours later and a noisy car drove straight into Toys Ahoy!
Out jumped a clown with a silver foil wig and red nose.

"Drowsy from Clown Town at your service, Joy," he said.
"Sorry I'm late, I got drowsy and nodded off again."

Joy tutted and showed Drowsy the annoying toys.

"Now, you're sure they're not rowdy?" asked Drowsy.

"Stop being a coward and sort them out," growled Joy.

"Hi toys, I'm Drowsy the Clown, so no frowns or scowls, eh?" He started juggling the clubs, but most fell to the ground. The scowling owl scowled, and the cow went, "bow-wow".

Add either **oi** or **oy** to each set of juggling balls to make a word from the story. Write each word under the balls.

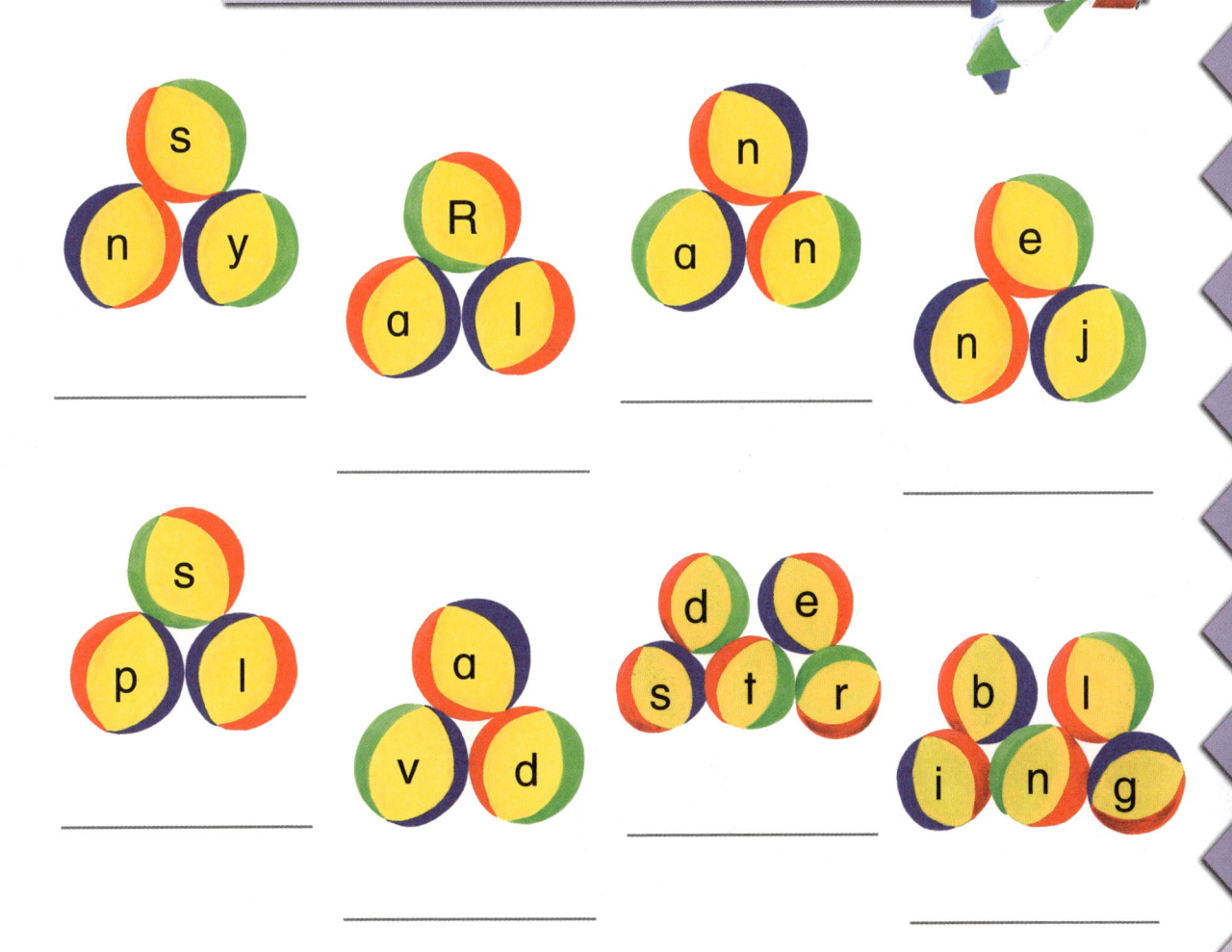

noisy

Royal

annoy

enjoy

spoil

avoid

destroy

boiling

"Best avoid juggling," said Drowsy, "but my jokes will wow the crowd."
"Why did the football referee send the chicken off?" he asked.
"Because it was a fowl! Foul…fowl…get it?" Drowsy bowed.
The owl and cow made no sound, and the ball didn't bounce around.

Drowsy told three more bad jokes,
then not another sound.
He fell asleep telling his own poor jokes,
and now lay on the ground!

Joy woke Drowsy up,
her eyebrows forming a frown.

"Don't glower or scowl, Joy,
I vow to sort these toys out."

"This is my secret weapon,"
said Drowsy, showing Joy a yellow flower.
"My squirty flower always gets a laugh –
it has magic powers."

10

Drowsy the clown's jokes are going wrong. Replace the underlined words with ones from the list so that the jokes make sense.

cat   cows   boy   confuse   pigs   toilet

1. Where do <u>sows</u> _____ watch films?
   At the moooo-vies!

2. What do <u>wigs</u> _____ put on their cuts and grazes?
   Oink-ment!

3. How do you <u>amuse</u> _____ a school bully?
   Put him in a round room but say there are ten pound coins in the corner!

4. Doctor, doctor, I keep thinking I'm a <u>boiler</u>! _____
   Hmm, you do look a little flushed!

5. Can I have a pair of brown trousers for my little <u>voyage</u>? _____
   Sorry, madam, we don't do swaps!

6. Roy: "Did you put the <u>towel</u> _____ out?"
   Troy: "No, it wasn't on fire!"

Drowsy's flower shot water past the owl, but it kept its scowl.
It then squirted some custard near the cow, which said, "meow."

"Looks like I need MAX power on my flower, Joy."
As Drowsy spoke, he squirted the flower at her and not the toys.

"**Watch out!**" shouted Joy, but it was too late.

His flower drowned Joy in thick custard as slimy as oil.
Joy was so annoyed, she thought her blood would boil!

"Whoops! Sorry, no need to get annoyed," shushed Drowsy.
Joy glowered and stomped off to take a shower.
Drowsy mopped up the slimy custard with a towel.

12

Each of these words has at least one shorter word hidden inside. See if you can spot all the shorter words and write them out.

voice _____

voyage _____

frown _____ _____

boycott _____ _____

blown _____ _____ _____

coward _____ _____ _____

boiler _____ _____

browse _____ _____

poison _____ _____

_____

"Time for a pow-wow," said Drowsy to a now clean Joy.
"A pow-what?" scowled Joy. She was still annoyed with this clown.

"A pow-wow – a meeting to think up a plan or a ploy," said Drowsy. "There must be a way to stop these toys from being so annoying."

"Couldn't you threaten the toys?" asked Joy.
"With drowning or poisoning or boiling them in oil?"

Drowsy scowled,
"Joy, destroying toys is not allowed!"
Joy frowned and felt bad.
How could she think of destroying toys?

Suddenly, Drowsy pulled out a coin on a string and put on a gown.
"I will put the toys in a trance and then ask them things."

Some words sound similar when read out loud, but have different meanings. Can you circle the right word to make each sentence correct?

The clown started to bough/bow.

A small boy/buoy handed back his toy.

It's just not allowed/aloud.

My squirty flower/flour always gets a laugh.

It was because the chicken was a fowl/foul!

They're not rowdy, you cowered/coward.

I fear these annoying toys may conker/conquer us.

Weather/Whether you like it or not, this cow goes "meow".

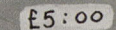

Drowsy swung the coin
in front of the brown cow.
The cow's eyes closed
and it started to lie down.

"How come, brown cow, you don't go moo?" asked the clown.
"But all the time go oink, meow or bow-wow?"

"I don't know," said the cow
in a quiet voice.
"I think it's because I like
a choice of noises."

"Well done, Drowsy, Drowsy…DROWSY!" cried Joy.
But it was no good. Drowsy was now in a trance himself!
In a daze, he tripped over the brown cow and fell down.
Off flew his foil wig, red nose and gown.

Destroy is an amazing word. More than 25 other words can be made from the letters inside it! See if you can spell out the following words from its letters, using the clues to help you.

_____ a colour

_____ what pigs live in

_____ when something like food turns bad

_____ the opposite of wet

_____ the past tense of the verb, tear

_____ a pretty flower

_____ what you should do when you're tired

_____ how it feels when you hurt yourself

_____ a tale like Joy's Annoying Toys

_____ the black rubber things on a car's wheels

Joy helped Drowsy up and handed him his clown's nose. There was a tiny bag of silver powder inside it.

"Oh great, Miss Royal, we now have a ploy," shouted Drowsy.

"This is magic clown powder with extra power. This will stop the toys from being annoying."

"You mean you had this powder all along?" growled Joy.

"Boy, I'm sorry, Joy," blushed Drowsy. "Annoyingly, I forgot!"

He prowled around the toy shop, sprinkling clouds of powder. "I vow this will work," he said in a nervous voice. Joy had to wait and see. She had no choice.

18

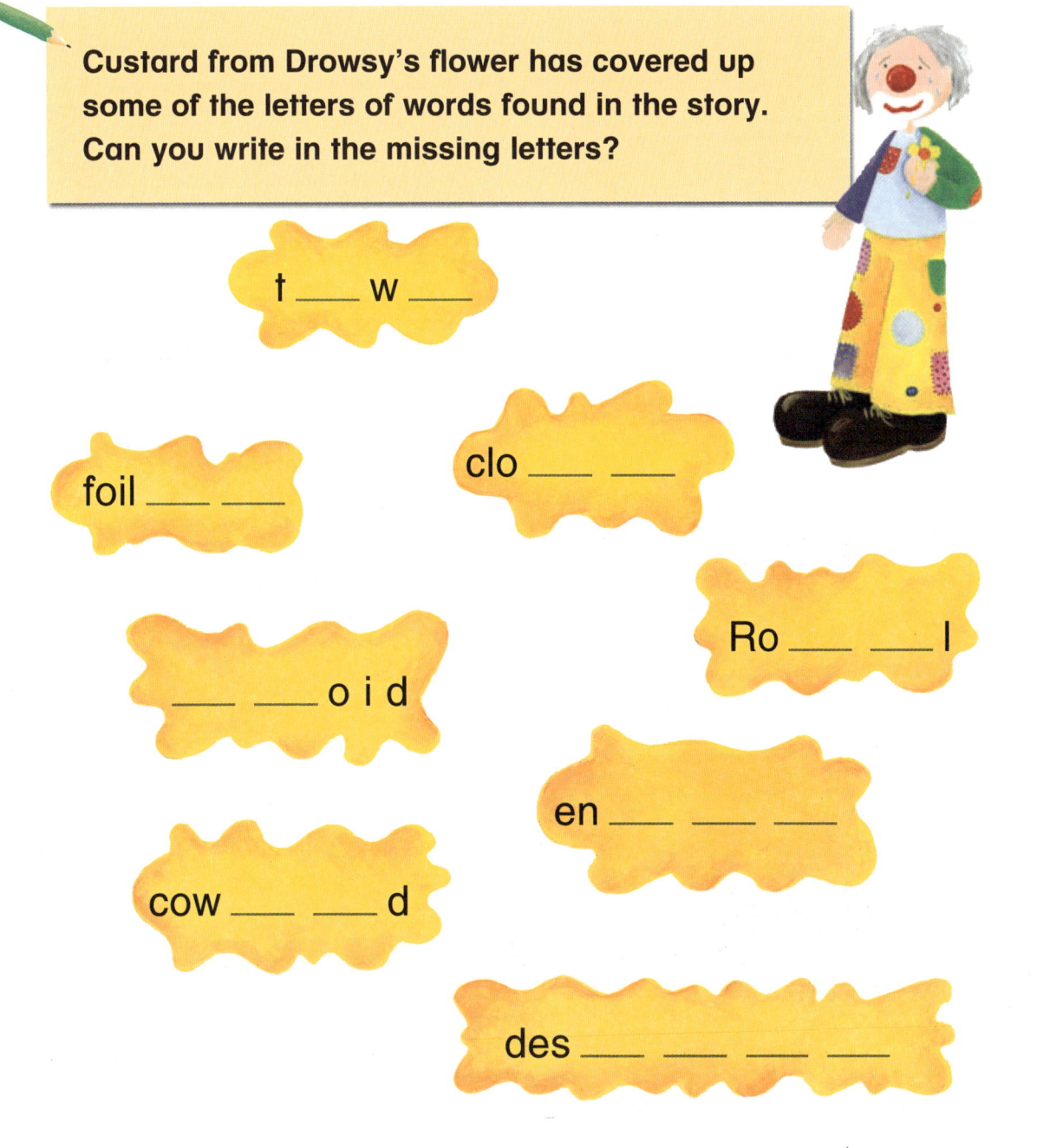

Custard from Drowsy's flower has covered up some of the letters of words found in the story. Can you write in the missing letters?

t ___ w ___

foil ___ ___

clo ___ ___

Ro ___ ___ l

___ ___ o i d

en ___ ___ ___

cow ___ ___ d

des ___ ___ ___ ___

19

Drowsy's clown powder really did have extra power.
First, the ball started bouncing up and down. **Wow!**
Then, the owl's face lit up with a smile instead of a scowl.
The cow made two oinks and, like a dove, went, "coo",
then it shook Joy's toy shop with an almighty "**m o o o o o o o o o !**"

Joy handed the boys back their toys to enjoy.
Drowsy clowned around and made them laugh with joy.

Drowsy's clowning around even made Joy no longer frown.
She turned to thank him, before he set off back to Clown Town.
He lay asleep on the ground. What a drowsy clown!

Now you have read the story of Joy's Annoying Toys, see if you can answer the questions below.

1. What was Joy's surname? _____

2. Which town did Joy ring for help with the annoying toys? _____

3. What was the name of Joy's shop? _____

4. How many jokes did Drowsy tell before falling asleep? _____

5. What colour was Drowsy's squirty flower? _____

6. What happened to Joy when Drowsy set his flower to max power? _____

7. What did Drowsy swing to put the cow in a trance? _____

8. What was inside Drowsy's clown nose?

_____

Answers

Page 3

uncoil – boil
boy – enjoy
choice – voice
android – avoid
joint – point
town – frown
flower – power
noise – toys

Page 5

pool (long)
crook (short)
good (short)
shook (short)
soon (long)
loose (long)
soot (short)
stood (short)
tooth (long)
school (long)

Page 7

Joy sold (noisy) toys.
The (spoilt) toys annoyed Joy.
There was a (cuddly) owl.
I'm scared of (rowdy) toys.
He fell asleep telling his own (poor) jokes.
There was a (tiny) bag of powder inside it.
Drowsy mopped up the (slimy) custard with a towel.
In a daze, he tripped over the (brown) cow.

Page 9

noisy
Royal
annoy
enjoy
spoil
avoid
destroy
boiling

Page 11

1. cows
2. pigs
3. confuse
4. toilet
5. boy
6. cat

Page 13

voice – ice
voyage – age
frown – row, own
boycott – boy, cot
blown – blow, low, own
coward – cow, war, ward
boiler – boil, oil
browse – brow, row
poison – is, on, so, son

Page 15

bow
boy
allowed
flower
fowl
coward
conquer
Whether

Page 17

red
sty
rot
dry
tore
rose
rest
sore
story
tyres

Page 19

town
foiled
clown
Royal
avoid
enjoy
coward
destroy

Page 21

1. Royal
2. Clown Town
3. Toys Ahoy!
4. four
5. yellow
6. she was covered in custard
7. a coin on a string
8. a bag of extra power clown powder

23

Published 2005
Letts Educational, The Chiswick Centre,
414 Chiswick High Road, London W4 5TF
Tel 020 8996 3333   Fax 020 8996 8390
Email mail@lettsed.co.uk
www.letts-education.com

Text, design and illustrations © Letts Educational Ltd 2005

Book Concept, Development and Series Editor:
Helen Jacobs, Publishing Director
Author: Clive Gifford
Book Design: 2idesign Ltd
Illustrations: Susie Thomas, The Bright Agency

Letts Educational Limited is a division of Granada Learning.
Part of Granada plc.
All rights reserved. No part of this publication may be reproduced, stored in a retrieval system, or transmitted, in any form or by any means, electronic, mechanical, photocopying, recording or otherwise, without the prior permission of Letts Educational.

British Library Cataloguing in Publication Data
A CIP record for this book is available from the British Library.
ISBN 1 84315 489 7

Printed in Italy

Colour reproduction by PDQ Digital Media Solutions Ltd, Bungay, Suffolk NR35 1BY